Golden Retriever Training Book for Beginners

The Comprehensive Golden Retriever Puppy Training Guide, Which Includes Step-By-Step Instructions, Common Behavioral Problems and 7 Things to Avoid When Training Your Golden Retriever

By

Jason Kayle

Disclaimer Notice:

Please note the information contained within this document is for educational and entertainment purposes only. All effort has been executed to present accurate, up to date, and reliable, complete information. No warranties of any kind are declared or implied. Readers acknowledge that the author is not engaging in the rendering of legal, financial, medical or professional advice. The content within this book has been derived from various sources. Please consult a licensed professional before attempting any techniques outlined in this book.

By reading this document, the reader agrees that under no circumstances is the author responsible for any losses, direct or indirect, which are incurred as a result of the use of information contained within this document, including, but not limited to, — errors, omissions, or inaccuracies.

Contents

Introduction

I want to thank you for choosing this book, 'Golden Retriever Training Book for Beginners - The Comprehensive Golden Retriever Puppy Training Guide, which Includes Step-by-Step Instructions, Common Behavioral Problems and 7 Things to avoid when Training your Golden Retriever.'

Did you just get a dog home? Are you ready to train him? Well, you're in the right place because we know just how important good training is. Few will argue with the fact that a dog is a man's best friend. This unique bond can be traced back to hundreds of years. Dogs remain loyal until their end and are always a source of joy to have around.

Anyone with a dog knows just how special the bond between man and dog can be, but with the pleasure of this special companion comes some responsibility. It is important to train your little puppy when he becomes a part of your home.

Golden Retriever Training Book for Beginners

In this book, we will deal with one of the friendliest species, the golden retriever. Retrievers are like golden balls of sunshine in our lives. They're extremely easy to please and follow you around everywhere possible, but they're also quite silly and need to be given some basic training in order to have them behave well.

When you first bring a puppy in, you will see that he tends to pee anywhere he pleases and might chew on your favorite pair of shoes too. This is why training is necessary in the first few months and that is exactly what we will help you do. You don't have to shell out a ton from your wallet and pay some strangers to do it. It can easily be done at home and will help you create a stronger bond with your dog.

By the time you are done following all the steps here, your puppy will be house- trained and won't bite everything they can get their teeth into. In fact, you will teach your retriever some neat little tricks that can be quite useful as well.

This book has been put together for you to better understand a golden retriever's usual tendencies and learn how you can make them more domestic. There are many different ways to do this, and we will tell you the simplest ways to save you time and effort.

You love your little pooch already but when he learns to obey commands and works on his silly ways, you will love your dog even more than you did before. You do not have to worry about spending hours teaching him or cleaning after him. You just need to invest a little time every day using the tips from this book and your golden retriever will be the picture of perfection.

So, what are you waiting for? Read on and start your journey of training your little golden retriever. I thank you once again for choosing this book; let's proceed.

Chapter One: Understanding your Golden Retriever

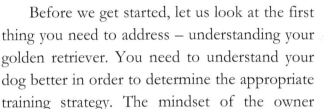

Before we get started, let us look at the first thing you need to address – understanding your golden retriever. You need to understand your dog better in order to determine the appropriate training strategy. The mindset of the owner should be such that they can fully take care of a new puppy.

Golden retrievers have their own unique behavior and characteristics, which set them apart from other breeds of dogs. They are a very loving type who may be naughty, but are quite easy to train. In fact, with the right training and trainer, they thrive in their routine. We will teach you how to understand their mind and get accustomed to, or change some things. Your own mindset needs to be patient and persistent in order for the training to actually work.

Unique Characteristics and Needs of Golden Retrievers

Understanding more about the normal temperament and behavior of your dog will help you get started. The golden retriever has one of the most family- friendly dispositions amongst most breeds. They are usually extremely cheerful and demonstrate affection quite easily. You will notice how they easily come when you call them, and follow you or your family around all the time.

Retrievers are very sociable creatures and not just to your family. They will generally be welcoming to any new people they meet as well. You don't need to worry about your dog intimidating any guests that come over either. Their bark itself is a friendly greeting and not angry, but you can trust their protective dog instincts in case of certain situations as well.

A golden retriever demonstrates a friendly and enthusiastic behavior even when he grows older and not just as a puppy. This type of behavior is endearing but sometimes might cause some trouble. This is why it is important to train them early on. They get easily distracted so it might be a little challenging unless you manage to stay patient. Persistence is key to changing your retriever's natural tendencies.

You also need to remember that retrievers are quite healthy as they grow up and have some strength. They are sweet dogs but might try to get rid of the leash you put on so keep a firm grip. Another habit you will have to deal with is that they love having something to chew on. They try to grab anything that catches their attention and tend to chew them out.

It is also not a problem if you already have another dog in the house. They are welcoming and peaceful with other animals. They mingle well and play together. Retrievers can generally keep themselves entertained so you don't have to keep playing with them; however, they are easily upset if you leave them alone so try to avoid that.

Golden retrievers are smart dogs and, with a little training, you can teach them some good habits and neat tricks that will impress everyone.

Common Behavioral Problems of Golden Retrievers

In order to change his habits, you need to consider all the behavioral tendencies of a golden retriever. Although their disposition is very friendly, they have some problems that may cause problems for you.

Firstly, they are highly energetic, especially when they are young. As puppies and sometimes even when they are grown, they tend to jump on people as soon as they meet. If your new puppy jumps around the house, you might find a lot of broken things over the next few days. Their behavior won't intentionally harm anyone, but accidents may happen so, if you have a toddler, try to be more careful. In such cases, it is better to adopt a grown retriever that has a more easy-going nature. They will be more careful and are easier to handle. As adults, golden retrievers have a more settled behavior and behave more calmly.

Another thing to consider is that they need regular activity and exercise. They need a regular routine of exercise in order to deal with their high level of energy. They were developed as hunting dogs so it is in their nature to be athletic. If you don't let them move around enough, they get bored and might behave badly in retaliation.

Shedding is a common characteristic amongst furry dogs. Considering their size and the density of their fur coat, you have to deal with a lot of shedding as they grow older. You will just have to deal with it. There might be a lot of fur on your clothes and furniture moving forward so you need to constantly clean. Giving them a brush through outside the house will help you control a little bit of it.

They also have some body odor that you will notice initially. Over time, you get used to it and you can try some other tricks to reduce the strength of the odor. Their odor and shedding make them difficult to deal with for a person with allergies.

One of the downsides to keeping a golden retriever is that they tend to get sick fast.

Retrievers have many diseases that they have to deal with. Unless you take proper care of them, you could lose them at an early age. Generally, a healthy golden retriever will live for at least 10 to 13 years, but many are lost around 7 or 8 if they are sick. Some of the diseases common to retrievers are bone disease, heart disease, and cancer, etc. There are ways to avoid these as much as possible and keep your dog healthy and thriving.

How a Dog's Mind Works

Communicating with your golden retriever

When you adopt a golden retriever, you need to know how to communicate with him. This will help you build a bond with him and also enforce some basic rules for him. You also need to keep in mind the past of the dog you adopt. If you get a newborn puppy then it is easier to start fresh and train him. If your retriever was adopted or rescued when he is older, you need to keep his past experience in mind. Try to learn more about him so that you know how you can communicate with him. Dogs that had a rough time before might be a little more difficult to deal with but just need some extra care. This is why communication is key. Dogs are more perceptive than they appear to be.

V o i c e

One of the first ways to communicate with your dog is using your voice. The tone of your voice, as well as the volume, will have an impact on them. You need to remember how amplified their natural hearing is so if you raise your voice at them, it can actually be very scary. Retrievers are very sensitive and will be affected more than others by any harsh tone, words or actions. It can leave a negative impact on them in the long run. This is one of the reasons why they stay scared for a long time, even if a tiny thing scares them as a puppy. They do not recover easily. Even if your dog is driving you crazy, you need to exercise calm. They respond well to low and slow talking. If your tone changes, they will instantly notice. Their own voice can be different when they express different emotions. Their bark is different when they are scared or anxious from when they are just excited about something. You need to discern the difference between these to understand him better.

Hands

Using your hands to communicate or signal your dog will also work. They use body movements amongst themselves so will be receptive to yours as well. When you are training them, using your hands will actually assist you in making them understand what you want. Many practices use hand signals to communicate with dogs and it will improve the rapport between you and your retriever as well. Training retrievers with hand motions will also be helpful in the future when they might lose their hearing. Dogs might also lose their hearing with age, just like humans, so these hand signals will help you communicate with each other later on.

Scents

Golden retrievers are born with a keen sense of smell. They use their nose first in most things, especially to judge if they should eat something or not; however, their habit of smelling makes it difficult to take them on a walk since they get excited and want to sniff at every new object that catches their attention. Dogs also tend to sniff each other when they first meet, like a type of greeting and judging of the other animal. You will also notice that they come up and smell you when you return home. They can actually tell if you played with another dog and will be very curious about it. They use their sense of smell to help train as well.

B o d y

Dogs primarily use their body to communicate. They exhibit many different types of emotions by their posture and movement. When they are scared, they tuck their tail in between their legs. If they want to be assertive, they will stand stiff and pull their ears back. While playing, they stay ready by bending their frontal part down while their rear end is up in the air. Studying your dog's different body movements will help you understand what they are trying to communicate over time. They are also responsive to yours so do not assert yourself in a violent or threatening way.

Retrievers, being sensitive, will shy away from you if you try to assert power over them in a harmful way. Use your body to show affection and excitement when you play with her. This will help her grow happier and stay healthier. This type of communication is especially important if you adopt a dog that was abused before. They will notice your physical behavior very closely and react accordingly.

Expressions

Golden retrievers have one of the most expressive faces and you can easily understand their emotions if you pay attention. When they are happy, their ears are relaxed and their mouth is usually half open, while their eyes have a soft look. At this point, they are completely relaxed. When they are excited, their ears perk up more and they wag their tongues out. If their teeth are bared, they are usually anxious or angry. The same way you can read him, he can also see a lot from your expressions. Retrievers can really empathize if you are sad or crying and the feelings even seem to transfer to them. They will also understand if your expression displays anger and this will make them be vary or move away, so keep a check on exhibiting extreme negative behavior that can affect your dog.

If you don't understand a golden retriever's mind, you won't be able to connect with him or manage to stay with him for long. It would be hard to teach them anything unless you try to understand their natural tendencies. Keeping their inborn instincts in mind will help you understand how they behave.

Chapter Two: Understanding the Training Process:

Training for golden retrievers

Training a dog is a process and cannot be done in a day or two. It involves following some rules and taking some steps over time the same way it does with our own children. If you want your dog to learn how to behave, you have to behave a certain way too. Such things will demonstrate to him what he should and should not do. Before you start, you need to have a plan. Dog training is a process and you need to dedicate some time and effort into it. We will tell you what and how to do these things but it is up to you to actually do it.

How to Avoid Reinforcing Bad Behavior

It is easy to forgive that innocent face staring up at you. You will instantly forget what they did and just hope that it does not happen again, but not demonstrating your displeasure at certain behavior will just make them think that it is okay. Just like good behavior deserves rewards, bad behavior needs some punishment, albeit humane ones. When they do certain things like break a vase or chew your shoes, you need to sit them down and talk to them. Make them sit and refuse to play with them for a while to show that you did not like what they did. Usually, retrievers love to please you and will avoid doing the same thing in future once it gets through to them.

How to Keep Your Dog Interested In Training

Your golden retriever may be adorable, but you will notice how he easily gets distracted by anything that falls in his line of vision. This can be a problem during training. This why you need to find ways to keep him interested. One of the easiest tricks is to use treats to lure him. Dogs love eating all the time, even if they just had their meal. This is why treats will always grab their attention. Click training is another method used during training a dog.

To make him focus during training, find a corner or area in the house where no-one will disturb you or nothing will distract him. His attention needs to be completely on the exercise that you use for training or he won't learn.

Positive reinforcement will also work in your favor. If you scold your dog for not learning faster, he will just get bored and try to avoid you. If you praise him instead when he gets something right, he will be more willing to learn better and please you. Retrievers always want to please their owner and this will help you, but if you display stressful and aggressive behavior, they won't respond well to you. You need to maintain calm and show affection to your dog as long as he doesn't do something bad.

Another way to keep him interested is to keep each training session short. They have a short attention span so, beyond 5-15 minutes, they will lose interest and be unwilling participants. These sessions are also ideal for a person who does not have too much free time to train their dog every day. The only thing you need to remember is that a few sessions every week are necessary to see any changes. They will easily forget a single session.

Try keeping these things in mind when you are training your dog.

How to Avoid These 7 Bad Training Techniques

Training your dog is not as easy as it seems. There are many bad training techniques that will give you the opposite result of what you want or just make it a longer process. Let's take a look at some of the things you should avoid:

Don't delay the training

One of the first things you should remember is to start training him as soon as possible. You might lead a very busy life and put it off for later; however, it is ideal to start as soon as you bring your dog home. The older he gets without training, the harder it'll be to teach him good habits. One of the first things to start work on is house training or basic commands. Learning things like tricks can be done when you have more time.

Don't give up

Another mistake is not training your dog enough. Don't expect him to learn everything quickly. It might be a little frustrating, but just give 5 to 10 minutes every day to see him actually learn something. A single session is not enough for him to grasp a new concept.

Jason Kayle

Not one fit for all dogs

Don't assume that all dogs are the same. Different breeds and different dogs are individually different. One might take longer than another to learn something, while others might be faster. Some methods don't work for one, while others might, so try whatever works for your dog and be patient.

Consistency Matters

It is important to be consistent in training. If you are inconsistent, then it will cause unwanted behavior in your dog. Also, avoid taking out your temper on your dog. You might have had a rough day, but he won't understand why you shouted at him for something that is normally ok. Inconsistent is also visible when you reward your dog for doing something half-way. He won't understand what he actually needs to do to deserve a reward.

Avoid Being Impatient

Your dog will be with you for a long time and it takes time for them to understand things. If you get frustrated just because he takes extra time to learn something, it'll harm your entire process. Don't do each session for too long. This way you can try a little without getting mad at him.

Leave the Aggression Out

Do not use aggressive punishment. The key to training your dog successfully is positive reinforcement. Every time he does something right, give him a reward and praise him. If he does something wrong, scold him but with a patient tone. Retrievers are very sensitive and will not respond well to anger. Physical abuse like hitting or grabbing him will only have negative results.

The Right Thing at the Right Time

Timing is everything you need to scold or reward him at the right time according to his behavior. If you leave things for later, it'll not have the same impact. During training for any verbal cues or tricks it is important to keep timing in mind while you are teaching him. When you shout out a word at him, he should instantly be able to associate it with the desired action. When he does something bad like peeing on the carpet, you need to reprimand him at that very moment so that he knows what it was that he did wrong. This is why you need to pay attention to the timing of your actions as well.

Clicker Response Training

Clicker training is commonly used while training animals, including your golden retriever, and has been found to be quite effective. This method uses a reward marker to capture certain types of behavior. It is like capturing a snapshot of that particular moment. During dog training, reward markers are used to make the dog associate some successful behavior with a reward. This works as a positive reinforcement for him. It is based on classical conditioning or automated behavior. It is like a type of reflexive behavior that is learned. The sound indicates how that moment is when the dog does something right and he will remember it associatively. Clicker training is used as an alternative to using treats since too many treats will not be healthy for your dog, but it will work effectively just as well. Use the reward marker and then give your dog a treat to show him that he did something good. Just about any animal can be trained using clicker response training, which uses three steps to get the behavior, mark it and then reinforce it on the animal. Try it out on your retriever to see positive results.

Chapter Three:

House Training

House training a dog is important if you don't intend to keep him outdoors and we recommend that you don't. Adopting a dog is a responsibility and you need to show them the love and affection they deserve. Keeping them outside in a kennel, or just in the backyard all the time, is a way to shirk responsibility, but if you keep them inside, there are some habits that you need to eliminate. These are some of the first few things that you need to get started with:

Setting Up His Personal Area

Your dog needs his own space just like everyone else in your family. Find an area that you think would be suitable and accessible for him. It should be private in case there are guests over. Determine the location accordingly. Now, you can create a space like a playpen for your puppy to play in, or just a small bed in something cozy, like a basket. The bed should be large enough according to the age and size of your dog so that he can rest there cozily. Keep his favorite toys there so that he knows it is his area. Also ensure that it is a safe space away from anything that will harm him. Don't keep any lamps and such looming overhead, and don't make his bed in the kitchen since they will always be distracted by the food and will never rest. His bed should be someplace that he can easily climb into and get out of. Also, keep a bowl of water next to him that is always refilled.

Get Him Accustomed To His Name

Giving your dog a name means you need to get him accustomed to it. Keep calling his name out while you look directly at him. After a while, he will start understanding that it is his name and answer to your call immediately.

When You Are Not At Home

When you are not at home, you need to consider some things, especially if it is a puppy. Try to keep them in a crate or outside in the kennel if no-one is home. Small puppies can be confined in a temporary fence-like crate that gives them space to move around, but away from any objects or things they might spoil. For slightly bigger dogs, use an appropriate kennel that allows them to move a little and rest. While they are untrained, they might get into all sorts of mischief. They will also tend to use any surface available as a toilet, which is why supervision is necessary in the first few months. Once they are older, you can leave your retriever home alone without much thought if they are well trained, but if you are away from home for too long, make someone come and give them food and take them for a walk until you come back. If you go on a trip, get someone to keep your dog for a few days, or come and dog-sit until you return. Do not leave them uncared for, for too long.

Separation Anxiety

Some dogs get a condition known as separation anxiety. Since dogs are very attached to their owners, it is normal for them to be a little upset when they are left alone for too long. They are scared of being left alone forever. They start barking loudly and settle into a depressive state, but once they see their owner come back, they start acting a little normally again. Severe separation anxiety can be a serious problem and needs to be addressed professionally. We have explained this condition further on in the book.

Crate training

Crates are used to section off an area for puppies when you aren't home or if they are up to trouble. When they aren't properly trained, you need to keep them secured so that they don't get hurt or break your valuables either; however, if you are gone for too long, you might feel uncomfortable leaving them alone in a crate. In this case, try to get someone to check over them and take them for a break after feeding them.

Potty Training

Potty training is an important part of training your retriever. As puppies, they think they are allowed to urinate or defecate anywhere they want; however, if you don't teach them some signals your house will soon be a mess. In fact, you can use a bell for this.

Keep a potty bell tied on or near your door so that it is accessible for your dog. Install the bell and get your dog familiar with it using some treats. If he reaches out and rings it, praise him and give a treat. He should just learn how to use the bell at this stage.

The next time he pees or poops somewhere, bring him near the bell and ring it. Also, every time you take him outside for this purpose, make him ring the bell. After a while, he will start ringing the bell himself every time he wants to go out to pee. Even if he rings the bell too often, take him out every time to show him that it is for that particular purpose. Don't let him play around when you go out. If he has a particular spot that he always goes in, make him stand there and wait until he poops.

The potty bell is not the only method as you can try other potty training methods as well.

Welcoming Visits

Your retriever can be taught to behave very welcomingly when a guest visits. With the right training, they will be sitting at the door in anticipation and will greet your guests very nicely. Just use the right tone and command and he will learn not to jump on people, but welcome them as politely as a dog possibly could. There is a lot further on in this book to help you with this training. Unmonitored behavior can be quite unpleasant for guests who are not as fond of dogs as you are.

Welcoming a New Member of the Family (Babies, Kids)

If you have a newborn child, there is no reason to get rid of your retriever. They are the most family-friendly animals and will be your child's best friend. Keeping a dog will also help build your child's immunity. Make sure your dog is clean and has had all his shots just to take extra precautions. Introduce the new member to him and let him cautiously hang around for a while to familiarize himself. Retrievers are usually very good with babies and will learn to be careful and play. Just keep them under supervision while the baby is very small.

Introducing other family pets (cats, turtles, birds)

You might have other pets like a cat or some birds in your house. Introduce them to your new dog, but first keep a comfortable distance. Let them get used to each other and assign each his own space. Golden retrievers are friendly and get along with most animals, but they might just get a little overexcited when they first get introduced, so keep him calm and teach him to slowly play around with the other animal without causing harm. This is especially so when they grow bigger and might be a little careless.

Chapter Four:

Street Training

Leash Training

Leash training is an important part of dog training, especially when you take your dog out in public to play or for a walk. Many areas actually have laws that ensure you walk a dog only if he has a leash around his neck that allows you to control him. You need to consider that some people are even afraid of dogs and will not welcome a stranger's dog jumping on them without warning. To start with, you need to select and purchase the right leash for your dog. If your retriever is a small puppy, the size needs to be small and delicate so that it does not hurt him. A bigger retriever is quite sturdy so you will need a tight leash that will help you hold him.

You need to keep a leash around his neck in a way that he can't wriggle out of it but it is not too tight. Hold the leash a little loose when you walk so that he has freedom of movement but does not run away. This will be enjoyable for him, but you can pull him if he tries to run or jump on someone. Usually, dogs get distracted easily, especially when they are outside the house. If you see a squirrel or something, grab his attention and tell him to sit or pull the leash if he tries running. When you walk him on the leash, he will soon learn that if he pulls or lunges, it will only hurt him. This will train him to be more appropriately behaved around strangers.

Training to stay (with or without the leash)

Your dog needs to learn to stay in one place with or without the leash. He should be obedient and know when he cannot run around and play. The leash is important to demonstrate your power over him initially. Over time, release the collar and just use verbal commands to make him understand. While training him, reinforce good behavior with praise and show your displeasure when he does not listen. It can be dangerous if your dog does not obey the stay command sometimes. Take your time and practice with him to make sure he listens every single time.

Techniques for Walking Your Dog

It is important to try and take your dog for a walk every day. They need some regular exercise and feel too cooped up indoors for too long; however, it is not an easy feat since they get extremely excited as soon as they step out and you need to be able to control them. There are certain tips that will help you walk your dog without too much trouble:

- First, get a leash with a front clip harness. Dogs usually try to pull free at some time and, if they are strong, it will be difficult for you to grab them from running away. A front clip harness makes it easier for you to pull him back and control him as opposed to a back clip one. The latter actually makes it easier for your dog to pull free as he uses more back strength.

- Don't pull your dog's leash too tight, give him some freedom to move freely and try to keep pace. It is good exercise for you too. Let him sniff around and satisfy his curiosity. As long as you have him on the leash or trained well, he won't jump on people. Dogs get a lot of mental stimulation just from this act of sniffing so let him go about it slowly.

- More than anything, the basic training commands that you teach him at home are important. These will help you assert some control over any unwanted behavior that your dog exhibits while out on a walk. They should listen when you tell them to sit, stay or drop.

- Also, try to avoid using a retractable leash on your dog. These leashes have been known to cause a lot of injuries to the dog as well as owners or other people. These types of leashes don't give you proper control and actually break off quite easily as well. This can cause many unwanted accidents, especially if your dog is not well trained.

- Another basic thing to remember is carrying a waste collector. Your dog will usually poop when you take them on a walk, and it is necessary for you to clean up after him. They cannot do so themselves and it is your responsibility to take care of this. It is extremely unhygienic to leave the poop just because it is not your home. Your neighbors will be extremely put off by such behavior.

- Since they get excited during walks, they get tired and dehydrated as well. Carry some water to give them in breaks. They get overheated very fast so dehydration will hamper their body temperature. This is especially important during summer months.

Golden Retriever Training Book for Beginners

- For the safety of your dog, make him wear a tag with your details and his name on it. This way, just in case you lose sight of him, the finder will know whom to return him to. They can easily get in touch with you if you keep your updated information on a tag. If not, you might just lose your pet if it is too far from home, so avoid such unwanted scenarios with a little extra care.

- Carry some treats with you because they might get hungry if you are out too long, and also, because sometimes you just need to catch their attention and treats are the easiest way to do this.

- Golden retrievers will also prefer an area with grass to walk on rather than roads or pavements. Parks are cool and more dog-friendly with many others for them to play with. Pavements get heated fast and are not dog-friendly. Their body does not respond well to too much heat.

- Don't assume that all dogs like each other or that their owners will want yours to play with them. You should ask before you let your retriever get excited and approach another dog. It can sometimes be a little scary for those with small dogs if they see a huge retriever running towards them. If your dog is well trained and you let him greet the other dog slowly, both animals and owners can be comfortable.

What to do when coming across strangers and other dogs

Initially, when your dog is a puppy, you need to be more careful about how he behaves in front of strangers or other dogs. At this point, they are unfamiliar with any new faces other than you. If you take them out in public, either hold the puppy in your arms or put a larger dog on a leash. They should not be able to jump on or startle others. Until your dog is well trained, he needs to be more aware of what he does when he is outside. Sometimes, your dog may approach another dog in a friendly way but, if the other dog is aggressive, they could both end up getting hurt. This is why there are strict leash laws in most places now. You also need to be considerate of other people who might be scared of dogs.

If there are guests in your house, keep your puppy in a fenced area or keep them with you so that they do not disturb visitors. When you start training your dog and take him outside, make sure that he obeys the basic commands you taught him as this will ensure that they know when to stop or come back if you call. Basic command training is crucial in ensuring that your dogs socialize well.

Barking

Golden retrievers can get very excited when they see new faces or even hear them. Barking is one of the most common ways that retrievers communicate, but their bark can mean different things. You will be able to understand when they are excited to see someone, or want to show their displeasure. Too much barking can be a behavior problem so train him to stop barking when you give the verbal cue to stop. Their obedience training is important in ensuring that they listen to you in such circumstances. If your dog is on a leash and runs up to another animal and starts barking, give him a little tug. Try to pull him back and calm him down. If he keeps barking at another dog, the other animal will also start barking and it might break into a fight. Be cautious about the environment you let your dog into at least until he is well trained.

Training to not jump on people when they come over

By natural instinct, dogs tend to get overexcited and jump on people when they first meet them, especially if they like them. This can be entertaining for some people who love dogs, but there are those who will find it annoying. This is why you need to teach your dog not to jump on guests so as to not make them uncomfortable.

When you are training your dog, you need to remember that jumping and licking is just a way for them to interact with a new person. You need to find another way that they get attention and can greet the guest. Train your dog to sit when a guest comes, and allow them to pet the dog while he is sitting. If he has learned some tricks like handshaking and rolling over, allow him to display those and reward him with some praise. This will make him satisfied with the attention and act more calmly around your visitors.

Avoid shouting at your dog or physically pushing him as he will probably just jump back again. Sometimes, he might just think that you are playing with him and he won't take the command seriously. Also ensure that your guest knows that there is a dog in the house and will not be surprised by it. This way, they can be warned and stay calm when they meet your dog.

When you start training your dog, firstly, keep him inside a barrier so that he doesn't jump out until you open the door. This way, he will start getting used to seeing new people. You can allow the guest to carry a treat in their hand and greet your dog.

Another step is to teach him to sit. He should instantly listen to you when you ask him to sit. Barriers do not always work for dogs so training is more important. Once he learns how to sit on cue, have another person approach him from a little far away. Your dog will initially try to run up to that person when he notices them. You should instantly shout sit to him, and make sure that he listens. If he doesn't move forward and stays in place, give him a treat and praise him. If he does not listen, be firmer and teach him until he obeys the cue. Once he learns to stop, make the other person walk to him and crouch down, and then give the dog a treat and pet him. If he tries to jump on the person, this time tell them to move back and command your dog to sit again. Keep practicing this a few times a week until your dog learns how to greet people without jumping on them.

Chapter Five:

Socializing

In this chapter we have some tips for socializing a golden retriever. Dogs need company just like humans do. Although he will be just as happy staying with you all the time if he is given affection, socializing is important too. Your dog needs to play with others and know how to behave with people other than you. We will tell you some tips that will let him get better at this over time and be a friendly dog that everyone appreciates.

Firstly, take him for walks every day. It is good for his health and will keep him active. He needs to spend all that excess energy at least once a day. Over time, he will get used to the outside world and not act overly-excited or behave inappropriately when he goes out. Training is important for the initial phase of a puppy. Once they learn to obey commands faster, they will be easy to handle when you go outside. Walks help your dog get familiarized to other animals and humans as well. He won't get freaked out every time he comes across any unusual situations. He might have an innate curiosity, but he will know how to control the way he behaves with the right commands from you. Take different routes so that he learns to accept new scenarios more easily.

At first, keep him in check and just let him walk around with you. He should just observe other dogs and people at this point. Once he is more familiar with the environment, let him approach others. He can start with dogs he meets in the park and any people who want to greet him. The manners you teach him will be very crucial at this point. Most people won't appreciate a dog jumping on them and startling them. He should actually be able to obey commands like sit and give a handshake, even if they are given by strangers. This will make him much more approachable and likable.

Slowly, over time, your dog will be good at socializing with others. You need to avoid too much time outside since it will become a habit and make him restless in your home. Remember that training takes time so be patient. He will get adjusted in time and behave properly.

Chapter Six:

Obedience and Basic Commands

Some basic obedience commands will help you train your dog. This way, he will know what to do when you give him commands and behave well. Golden retrievers are fast learners so it should not take more than a few weeks, but persistence is key. It is also important not to overdo it. Don't try something for more than 5 minutes in a row since they will easily lose interest. Also, avoid being harsh or too physical. This kind of approach might actually hurt them and does not really incite them to behave well in future. They respond well to firmness, but need to feel affection as well.

Sit Command

Sit is an important basic cue to teach your golden retriever. Training your dog to sit is one of the easiest and basic commands that you need to deal with. He needs to associate the word "sit" with the action.

a) First, keep a few treats handy. Now take one in your hand and bring it near his nose so that he knows it is there.

b) Now keep moving your hand slowly up and down and see how his head goes up and down with it.

c) In a while, you will see that he sits by himself and that is when you have to say, "sit" and hand him the treat. The timing of your command is crucial. Use your hand to show him if he has to get up or sit down in order to get it right. Keep doing this a few times and he will know what the sit command means.

d) You can also keep noticing what he does the whole day and every time he sits, grab his attention by loudly saying "sit" and give him a treat. This trick might also work since he will expect a treat every time he sits down.

Some clever fellows might even cheat. They don't completely sit down and just hover ready to pounce on a treat. You need to make sure he is firmly down with his rear on the ground. Obedience is key before you treat him. Also, avoid pushing him into a sitting position by force if he doesn't listen. Some dogs will not respond well to this and won't learn either. If your training isn't working, try and observe when he sits by himself and instantly say, "sit" and praise him for doing it. He will soon learn to sit on cue. Actually, training them for the sit command is perfect before serving food or taking them out the door. These are when they are most willing to please you.

Lay Command

The lay command is important while training your dog manners. Once they start responding to it, you can command them to lay and calm down if they get hyperactive. In this position they are forced to stay still until you allow them to move around again. It allows them to relax from their excited state.

Golden Retriever Training Book for Beginners

a) Get some small treats that your dog likes. Get him in a quiet area so he can concentrate on the training.

b) Now, take one treat and hold it near his nose.

c) Once he looks at it, slowly move it down on the ground.

d) He should move down with it using his elbows and hocks. When he successfully does this, offer him the treat.

e) Repeat the above step and when he is more consistent in lying down, add the "down" verbal cue.

f) Say "down" clearly while you move the treat down and keep doing this a few times every day.

g) After a while, get rid of the treat and train him to lie down anytime you say "down."

Carry out this exercise a couple of times every day until you see results. As your retriever starts responding better to the cue, don't tempt him with treats and just teach him to follow the command, but reward him once in a while to reinforce good behavior. Also, change the location a few times so that he does not just associate this practice with a particular place.

Come Command

Teaching your dog to come as soon as you call out to him is necessary. This is especially so in cases of emergencies when you need his attention and he should immediately come at being called. This command will also help you to keep control over him when you take him out without a leash. If he is well trained, you can just call out to him if you notice him doing something undesirable. It is one of the easiest and earliest commands to teach your retriever while he is a puppy. Since golden retrievers have a very pleasing nature, they usually obey as soon as you call, but they also get distracted easily so it is important to train your puppy properly to avoid any trouble. While you train him, you need to keep your calm and never use an angry tone, just be firm. It might be frustrating at first, but do not show it to him, so 5-10-minute sessions should be good for you both.

a) Find an area that won't distract your dog. His attention should be on you.

b) Keep a toy or treat in your hand. This will make him want to listen to you. Hold the toy up as you say "come" in a clear voice.

c) Make some motion with your hand like calling him forward or tapping your knee. Try taking a step back as you motion him to move forward.

d) Once he comes near you, give him a treat and praise him a little.

e) First practice this with your dog on a short leash, then a long leash and finally without a leash when you see him getting better.

f) After a while, you need to stop giving treats so that he doesn't expect one every time you call. He needs to learn to come without any incentive.

g) Train him for a maximum of 15 minutes a day and do this at least three times a week.

Another thing to remember is that you should only ask your dog to come for a positive reason. Don't use the command for a punishment. This will make him reluctant to answer or obey when you call him again. The training with a treat or toy is to establish this as a positive experience for him.

Stay Command

Your dog needs to know when to stay in place if you ask him to. Just like he needs to learn when to come to you, your dog needs to stay if you command as well. This can be important when your dog gets involved in something dangerous and needs to be stopped. He needs to learn to be calm in certain situations and just obey you. This command is a little harder than some others, but not too difficult.

a) Use a long leash with a collar on your dog.

b) Now ask him to sit or lay. This helps if your dog is too energetic.

c) Now hold your palm out near him and firmly say "stay."

d) If he sits calmly and doesn't move, give him a treat.

e) Repeat this and say "stay" as you motion him with your hand.

f) Take a few steps back and see if he moves or stays.

g) If he still stays down then give him a treat again. If he moves, repeat the exercise.

h) Say okay to release him for the stay position.

i) Repeat the stay and okay commands until he gets used to it. Over time, try to make him sit for longer so that he gets faster in obeying.

j) Start trying the exercise from further distances over time and soon away from his line of sight as well. He should be able to listen and stop instantly.

After your dog starts obeying the command better, you should try practicing when there are more distractions nearby. This will show you that he can listen during different situations.

Leave Command

Your dog should automatically listen to you and drop or turn away from something if you tell him to "leave it." This command is important when you see him approaching something like your shoes to chew on, or even plants that are in your garden. If you ask him to leave it, he should be able to easily turn away after training for a while.

a) First, find an area where he will concentrate on you and not get distracted by other things.

b) Now take a treat in your hand and show it to your dog.

c) When you see him approach it and it has

grabbed his attention, close your hand over the treat and say "leave it."

d) He will initially rub his nose on your hand and try to lick and get it. When he stops doing that and moves back, praise him and give him a different treat.

e) The one in your hand should still be closed inside. Be firm about not giving him this treat.

f) First, give him a treat as soon as he backs off, and then test his patience over time to see how long he can wait until you willingly give it to him. He needs to learn to be patient.

g) After doing this a few times, keep the treat on the floor away from your dog and tell him to leave it as soon as he is near it. Repeat until he stops.

h) Repeat the exercise a few times until he understands that he needs to leave the treat alone. At first, he will understand that he will get another treat instead, but slowly the command will be imbibed in him.

i) After a while, you can start using this command for other objects as well and he will learn to leave them alone.

Chapter Seven:

Obedience Advanced Commands

Drop Command

The "drop" command is also an essential part of training your golden retriever. This can actually save him from harm on many occasions. Dogs might unknowingly swallow things like medicine, which can harm them immensely. First of all, such things should always be stored away from the reach of children and pets, but just in case you see them near any, they should immediately drop it if you command them. Even if it is not something that serious, you just might not want them to drop something they shouldn't be playing with. The drop command is one of the fastest that dogs will learn most of the time.

a) First, offer one of his favorite toys to him and tell him to take it.

b) Once he grabs it with his mouth, let him play a minute and then hold a treat near his nose.

c) He will naturally choose food over a toy and drop the toy.

d) Once he drops it, give him the treat. Repeat these steps a few times until he responds faster.

e) After this, add the command "drop it" firmly while you hold up the treat.

f) Slowly increase the distance between the treat and your dog as you repeat this exercise over the next few days.

g) Once you see him resounding better to the drop command, try it without any treat. When he responds by dropping the toy, praise him and offer a treat.

Once your retriever grasps the drop command, he will know instantly to drop anything if you command him.

Go to places

Now, let's try to teach him how to go somewhere when you tell him to.

a) First, choose a place like his bed that you want him to go to.

b) Your dog should be trained to stay down when you ask him to by now.

c) Stand near the bed with your dog with a treat in your hand and say "go there" using the treat as an indicator.

d) He will follow the treat and sit on the bed.

e) Do this from a few feet away after a while. Soon, he will understand that you are telling him to go to the bed each time. Command him to stay down on the bed for a while each time you practice this so that he knows he has to stay there for a while.

f)   After a while, practice with other places.

Go to people

Let's teach him to go to people now. He will usually tend to follow his owner around, but he needs to play with others as well.

a)   Find someone to practice this with. Keep a few treats handy.

b)   Both of you stand on opposite sides of the room.

c)   Motion your dog to come to you first. By now, he should know when to "come" when you call.

d)   Then tell him to "go to him" and motion towards the other person who should be holding the treat. The treat will make your dog willing.

e)   Let the other person give him the treat when he goes.

f)   Now, call him back and repeat the exercise.

g)   Use treats the first few times and then just use the verbal command. He will get used to it and learn to go to someone else when you ask him to.

Your dog will soon learn to go and play with other people as well. His training should emphasize some basic manners like not jumping on them in such cases.

Roll Command

By now, your retriever probably knows when to sit, stay or lay down on verbal cues. Now you can teach him a trick to roll over. It can be something fun to do while playing, or just to show your friends how smart your dog is. It will also help you when you need to check his body for any injuries or infections; otherwise, it can be hard to get him to stay in such a position.

a)   Take a few treats that your dog likes.

b)   Command him to get into the lying down position.

c)   Move the treat near his nose so that he is aware of it. Now move your hand towards his shoulder and see that his head is moving with it as well.

d)   Now slowly move the treat near his back. He should flip over while trying to follow his treat. Repeat this until he rolls on to his other side and give him a treat as soon as he does.

e)   Repeat this a few times.

f)   Then add the verbal cue and say "roll over" and soon as he's about to turn and then you praise him.

g)   Remove the treat after a while and just use the cue to indicate what you want him to do. Practice this once in a while so that he doesn't forget.

h)   Also, try to use hand signals to motion him while he turns over. Over time, he will learn to roll over just with you motioning that signal.

It might take a while, but teaching him to roll over will be a fun practice. Golden retrievers love pleasing you so they will learn as quickly as they can.

Heel

Sometimes you need to get him to heel. These steps will help you make him understand this command:

a) First, make your dog sit near the door and wait for a while. While sitting, he already knows he has to listen to you further when you're looking at him.

b) Now, place his leash around him and give the okay command to get up so that he can stand.

c) Go out the door with him.

d) Why walking, always try to have your dog on your left.

e) Now, say "heel" and walk before him. He will follow you but you should turn and walk back again. He has no choice but to turn with you. Say "heel" when he does and praise him for being a good dog.

f) Keep walking with him and when you feel him pulling too much on the leash, turn and say "heel" again. Praise him when he follows.

g) You need to repeat this until he understands you.

h) Now, just keep walking and say "heel" without turning. He should stop and turn by himself.

i) After a few days of practicing this, he will know when to stop and you will have better control over him outside.

It is important to teach your dog to heel because they tend to get overexcited and leap forward when you take them outside. Teaching him to heel means he will know when he has to stop.

Beg

Teaching your dog to beg is another neat little trick you can try.

a) Keep a few of your retriever's favorite treats handy.

b) First ask him to sit. When he is in the sitting position, place a treat near his nose.

c) Now say "beg" to him.

d) He will reach out to grab it with his mouth but move it high so that he has to move up as well.

e) He should now be on his heels with his front paws off the ground and begging you to give it. As soon as he is in this position, say "good boy" to him and give him the treat.

f) If he isn't in that position, just keep practicing until he does it and don't give him the treat until then.

g) Repeat this a few times every day.

h) Once he starts getting into the begging position fast, stop handing out treats. He will still remember the command and get into position so praise him every time he does it.

Praise is necessary to reinforce good behavior in your retriever.

Bow

Dogs look very cute when they perform little tricks like bowing. They know it'll get your attention and he will love the praise as well.

a) Keep some treats available for this training.

b) Make your dog stand now. If he hasn't learned to follow this command, teach him this first.

c) Now take a treat near his nose and slowly move your hand down his body. He will follow the treat with his nose until his elbows are on the ground. His rear will still be up in the air. If he pulls his entire body down, use your other arm under his stomach to indicate he should push his posterior up.

d) Praise him and lure him up again. Give him the treat then.

e) Now, take another and make him get back into position. Use the cue "bow" when he starts moving down and praise him once he gets up to stand again.

f) Keep doing this until he knows that he has to bow and stand every time you cue him.

Don't try this trick on him for more than 5 minutes a day or he will get bored soon.

Shake

Who doesn't love it when a dog shakes his paw with you? Your retriever will look like the most adorable gentleman there is.

a)   Make your dog get into the sitting position.

b)   Now, hold up a treat to him so that he knows it is there but close your fist over it before he takes it.

c)   Move your hand down towards his paw. Try to get him to move his paw. If he does this, praise him. He will usually try to put his paw over your fist with the treat.

d)   Open your fist to give him the treat when he moves his paw at you, but shake it with your other hand first. Praise him and then let him have the treat.

e)   The first few times you should reward him, even for a little bit of progress.

f)   When he keeps lifting his paw, add the "shake" word as a verbal cue.

g)   Give treats in intervals. He should know that he wouldn't get a treat every single time he does it but that there is still a chance.

Practice this for a few times everyday. Too much will make you both frustrated and tired. A little progress every day is more than enough.

Begin Retrieving

Teaching your dog to retrieve or fetch is going to be quite simple since they love playing, but it will take a while for them to understand the cue.

a)   Take a toy that your dog likes playing with. Get him to sit and see that it is in your hands.

b)   Throw the toy away and ask him to get it. He will usually run after it. Praise him if he gets it and motion for him to come back.

c)   If he doesn't chase it, you should run after it to show him what he should be doing as well. He will mostly follow you.

d)   If he gets the toy back to you, give him a reward.

e)   Add the cue "fetch" after the first few times. He will initially just perform the exercise to get a treat, but then he will get used to it and keep playing just for the enjoyment.

Once he learns how to fetch, your dog will easily obey this command because retrievers love to play and have a lot of energy. They enjoy chasing after objects and bringing them back to play again.

Chapter Eight:

Common Behavioral Problems

Let us talk about some of the specific behavioral problems of golden retrievers. If you make an effort to understand some of their puzzling behavior, it will help you to deal with them in future.

Trust

Golden retrievers will usually be very forthcoming and welcoming towards you, especially if they are puppies as they will easily welcome you as a friend; however, sometimes they won't. This happens more in the case of older dogs. If your retriever was adopted from the animal shelter, or had an abusive past, he will be much more self-protective. Their body and spirit are both harmed in such cases. Some homes take the dogs in, but do not care for them properly and might even abuse the animal. Until they are rescued, they know that they have to protect themselves. When they find themselves in a new environment, they will not open up so easily until you demonstrate that you can be trusted.

It is easy to spot untrusting behavior in dogs. They won't make eye contact with you. They shy away from physical contact most of the time. Some of them will actually react quite violently if you surprise them when they don't notice. It is not because they want to harm you; it is just their instinctive behavior. Such dogs won't want to play or engage like golden retrievers usually do. This makes you realize just how much they were hurt in their previous home or situation.

Be gentle with your dog if he seems to exhibit this kind of behavior. Before you set about to train them, first establish a relationship of trust. Let them do as they please for a while as long as it is not something harmful or destructive. Keep them away from other dogs that are aggressive. Show them love and affection as often as possible. Over time, you will see that they willingly follow you around or want to engage with you. Trust is very important in order to have a happy dog in your home.

Biting

Biting is one habit that your dog needs to learn to stop. Usually, retrievers are very friendly dogs and don't even bite strangers, but it is more prominent in them as puppies. Although biting is an instinctive habit, they need to know when they should or should not use their teeth. If you fail to instill this in them, others might get injured. In case of puppies, it is normal and not harmful since their bite is small and usually toothless. They use their teeth while playing with new things, but they also need to be shown that they have to stop. There are different reasons for your dog to bite.

Sometimes they will bite if they are scared and want to defend themselves. This is perfectly normal if someone shows violence towards them. Dogs are also very territorial and have a keen sense of danger; they might bite any stranger they see entering the property without a familiar face beside them. Some dogs however are too aggressive for unknown reasons and might bite just to show dominance. This type of behavior needs to be dealt with firmly. Bite inhibition can be taught through proper practices and socialization.

Chewing and Home Destruction

Chewing is an especially common trait amongst puppies when they are teething. Their mouth hurts and they want to bite things. This phase usually passes and you can deal with it by giving them some teething toys; however, in general, dogs like to chew. It is just a part of their nature. Give them a toy and they may love it, but they will still chew on it and try to tear it apart. Grown dogs usually tend to exhibit this kind of destructive behavior when they are bored or just anxious. It might sometimes also be out of curiosity when a new object catches their eye. Sometimes dogs just expend extra energy by getting rough with objects. One way to avoid this is ensuring he gets enough exercise every day. To avoid the destruction of your personal items, give your retriever enough toys to play with. Keep things like shoes away from his reach. In case your dog has the tendency to chew too much, keep him confined if you are not home. Supervision is necessary until you can correct this habit. If you see him chew on something he shouldn't, instantly reprimand him and motion that he should not touch it again. It might take time but they slowly learn.

Barking

Barking is something most dogs will do; however, there is a limit to how much is normal. If they bark too much and it is during all hours of the night, it is an issue, but first you need to understand why he is barking. Only then can you try to correct his behavior in a way that your neighbors would appreciate.

Sometimes your dog will bark just to get attention. His bark could indicate symptoms like anxiety or boredom as well. Dogs also bark more when they get very excited or while they are playing; however, if it is around night and not something he always does, pay attention to it as a warning. Dogs are very protective towards their owners and have a keen hearing sense. This allows them to sense danger quicker than we could realize it. If he just barks too much to get attention, try teaching him a few "quiet" commands to make him stop barking. You need to be patient while you do this, even though it might be a bit frustrating.

Hyper dog

Does your dog appear to be more hyper or energetic than others? Maybe he runs around too often and keeps jumping around but, most of the time it will just be too much energy if they haven't exercised or played for a while. In rare cases, hyperactivity can be a medical condition in your dog as well. You need to know the difference between the two in order to respond appropriately or take him to a vet.

As puppies, retrievers have a lot of energy

and are excited most of the time. This is why training is important in this initial stage in order to calm him down. Training and regular exercise will ensure that they use their excess energy in a good way.

Compared to some other breeds, golden retrievers require a little less activity. They will be satisfied with some appropriate play times in a day; hence, it is not so hard to prevent hyperactive behavior in them.

When your dog acts too hyperactively, he is usually looking for attention. Ignore him so that he does not get it. Don't look at him or shout out at him. At some point he will calm down by himself. You should act calm as well. Reward him when he behaves well and ignore him if he does not. This will give him an indication of the kind of behavior you will appreciate. Also, make sure that you are giving him the amount of exercise that he requires every day. Exercise is necessary for good health and mental stimulation. Your retriever will get bored and anxious if he has nothing to do all day. Good obedience training is also necessary for you to be able to control him if he overreacts sometimes. If you see that you can't change his behavior or he appears too erratic, it might be a good idea to take him to a vet or specialist for treatment.

Hard-Headed

Some dogs can be quite stubborn by nature or just in some situations. In such cases, it can be hard to deal with them or train them. First, you need to make sure that your stubborn dog responds to the name you have given him. You need to be patient and persistent when you deal with such a dog. Emphasize that you are the alpha and that he needs to listen to you. You cannot do this by using harsh words or actions. Just be firm and praise him only when he follows instruction. It might take a little more patience than others, but it is required if you want to see results. You need to gain their respect in order to make them listen to you.

Scared dog

Just like you, golden retrievers are also scared of certain things. Some of their fears are common amongst dogs, while some fears develop due to experiences. You can see that he is scared when he runs and hides, trembles, whines or even barks loudly. It is your responsibility to take care of him in these cases.

One of the common things that dogs are scared of is loud noise. This can be from a variety of sources. Thunderstorms may startle them and scare them a little. They can actually sense these approaching before humans do. One of the worst experiences for dogs is fireworks. Their sharpened sense of hearing makes the noise too loud for them to bear. They get very scared when they hear too many fireworks. Try to keep them away from such things and use medication if it is too much.

Retrievers are very sensitive and attached to their owners. While they can be independent, some develop separation anxiety. This makes them behave erratically if they realize you are leaving. You will notice how your dog barks a lot if you go out and close the door leaving him alone. They will behave normally when you return but, until you do, they remain quite upset. Many studies were done where videos were taken of dogs in the house while their owners were at work. This is why we recommend that they not be left alone for long hours; try a sitter or dog care.

Early socialization is also important to avoid certain fears in dogs. Try taking them for car rides with you or later on it will be hard to travel with them. New situations can sometimes be overwhelming for them. If your dog is scared of the stairs, carry him up and down a few times, then play with them and incite them to come down to you by themselves as well. Over time, it might help them get over it. Lack of socialization also makes dogs very wary of strangers. They react by barking loudly and baring their teeth. The new person might get injured as well if your dog gets too aggressive. New objects like vacuum cleaners can also scare your dog at first since he won't be familiar with it. Try to calm him down and show that it is not harmful.

Ultimately, you need to know that your dog has his own fears. If you see him exhibit such symptoms, try to help him through it or take the help of a vet. Extreme reactions might sometimes require sedatives in order to calm down your dog.

Sibling Issues

Sometimes, dogs don't react well to having siblings. A sort of sibling rivalry may arise in such cases and lead to unwanted behavior. There can be many causes for sibling rivalry, some get triggered over food and others fight for attention. Sometimes, it may arise even amongst the friendliest siblings by fault of the owner. Both dogs should get equal care and affection. In the case of food, give them healthy things that are recommended for their breed and not junk. This latter type actually triggers misbehavior.

There are some tips that will help you prevent or deal with this kind of behavior. Feed them separately in different bowls away from each other. They shouldn't eat each other's meals. Treat them the same way and don't be partial to one or the other. Ignore any attention-seeking behavior so that they know when they are behaving badly. Good training is required so that you can manage them when they get out of control. Teach them discipline so that they never break away while on walks or jump on strangers. Regular exercise and play will allow you to give them a push in the right direction.

How to handle problems with dogs and visitors

Socializing your dog is important in his training. If they don't get familiar with new faces and places, they might misbehave. Dogs with trust issues can also cause problems initially. In such cases, keep them away from guests until they are well trained. Let them out in the yard or take your guests to another room. Be firm with them and tell your dog to sit and play with his toys when someone is around. If he might jump on people, it might be okay to keep them on a leash for a while, but it is important to just train them over time and let them become friendlier with strangers.

How to stop leash pulling

Your dog will initially try to resist any leash you put on them. If you take them for a walk, they will use all their strength to pull away and get rid of your hold. Firstly, don't use retractable leashes since these break easily and make it easier for your dog to get out of. If he tries to pull the leash while you are on a walk, just stop and ask him to sit. Don't move until he listens and calms down. Move forward and let him start walking by your side again. If he pulls away again, just give a tug and stop again. He needs to realize that until he stops tugging on the leash you won't let him walk around as much as he wants. This will help him understand. Give him a treat when he walks companionably by your side.

Teach your unfocused dog to listen

Golden retrievers can get distracted very easily by things that catch their eye. It can be hard to teach or train them in such cases. Some are even more unfocused than others. To deal with this, find a quiet corner with nothing that will distract them while training. Don't let your kids or anyone else come and play at that time either. Their attention needs to be focused on you. Use treats or their favorite toy to help keep that focus on you. You cannot grab his attention if you try all this in a park or somewhere that has many distractions.

Fearfulness

Like we mentioned before, dogs have their own fears. You need to be compassionate and identify such behavior. Find out what he is scared of and try to avoid putting him in such situations or slowly get over the fear. Certain fears can be taken care of with training and affection. Some like the fear of fireworks need to be avoided since it scares almost all dogs. Try to make them feel comfortable with you and understand that you will protect them. Tools like earmuffs might muffle such loud sounds for them a little. Take help from professionals for more help with strong behaviors or fearfulness.

Loss of House-Training

Your retriever might suddenly revert to behavior he exhibited before training. He might be chewing things and urinating in random places too. There can be different reasons for this as well. One could be a medical condition that is affecting his mental state. Dogs also urinate to mark their territory. Another instance in which this is exhibited is if you leave them alone for a long time or even with someone else while you go on a trip. Golden retrievers, in particular, can get extremely upset when they are separated from their owners due to deep attachment. They might retaliate and ask for attention by behaving badly. This can be corrected by giving them a little extra care and affection. Sometimes they might just lose all good training habits if the people they stayed with did not enforce any rules. This will require some guidance from you again in order for him to rectify his behavior.

Dealing with Aggression with other Dogs, Cats or People

Aggression can stem in dogs due to many reasons. First, you should take them to a vet since it could be due to a medical issue. They will guide you in getting the condition treated. In general, aggressive dogs can be scary for people. They exhibit this behavior by baring their teeth wide and growling, jumping and biting people. This behavior might stem in older dogs that have a history of abuse. Some owners hurt their dogs instead of caring for them and this makes the dogs innately defensive to protect themselves. Sometimes a dog might just be aggressive if their parent was aggressive as well. Get professional help for this type of behavioral correction since it won't be easy.

Chapter Nine:

Exercise, Fit and Fun

Golden retrievers have a lot of energy and need regular exercise to stay fit both mentally and physically. They are also prone to numerous diseases so regular exercise is essential for them to stay as healthy as possible and live a full life. If you keep your retriever indoors all the time and don't take him for a run or play with him, it leaves him anxious. There is too much unspent energy that he can take out in unwanted ways and it will also leave him feeling depressed if you don't play with him. We have already asserted how sensitive retrievers are to our behavior so you need to keep this in mind. Exercise can be in the form of different activities and games that your retriever will enjoy. They will only do something that is fun for them and your job is just to make sure they get a little activity every single day.

Best way to exercise a golden retriever

Golden retrievers love playing and have a good amount of energy to spend. You need to make sure to give him enough exercise every day unless you absolutely can't. They can get antsy if they get too bored and have unspent energy. There are many ways in which you can exercise a golden retriever. Since they learn well, you can even train them to learn many new games or even run on a treadmill.

- One of the easiest ways to exercise your dog is taking him for a walk or run. He will willingly walk beside you and will enjoy the outdoors immensely. If he is well trained, you can even leave him out without a leash if it is allowed in that area. Keep the leash laws of some places in mind before you let go of your dog.

- Playing fetch is another commonly loved game by dogs. Carry a ball or toy that your dog likes and throw it for him to catch and get back to you. The fetch command can be very useful and fun when you play with him. Don't use objects like sharp sticks or anything that might injure your dog or someone else while you play. Softball is the easiest to play with. Fetch is easy to play in the house as well if you can go outside.

- If you enjoy hikes, you can take your retriever as well if the ground is not too hard for him. A soft trail will be appropriate for him or he could injure his paws. The hiking trail needs to be dog-friendly so check for that. Carry a lot of water and some food to replenish his energy during hikes. This exercise is a little harder than others and will require a lot of energy from him. After returning from hikes, give them a good bath and check for any fleas.

- Dogs love water if they are introduced to it early on. They catch on to swimming quite fast and enjoy it, especially on summer days when it gets too hot. Choose a small pool or one that is dog-friendly. Remove any collars or leashes from him when he goes into the water. Keep an eye out to make sure he is alright while swimming. They are natural swimmers and will make the most out of their time in the water. If your dog is still a puppy, don't let them into the water alone. Help them get used to it using a float if they appear too scared. They will soon get the hang of it.

- Many dogs have learned how to use a treadmill with some proper guidance. If you have a small house, it doesn't mean that you can't exercise your dog. A treadmill can be used for your dog, as well as yourself, but first, familiarize him with the machine for a few days. Let your dog watch you use it. When you turn it off, make him get up on it and sit for a while.

- Take him to a dog park as a special treat. There will be many dogs for him to play with and such places have activities especially for dogs to enjoy. It will give him a good workout just to run around with other dogs.

- You can also enjoy a game of hide and seek with him once in a while. Since retrievers are very curious; they actually keep playing until they can figure out where you are. Distract them and run and hide somewhere. Call out when you know they are far. They will keep sniffing around to look for you. Another variation of this game is hiding treats instead of yourself. Show him the treat and then go and hide it somewhere. His sense of smell will guide him to find it and, if he does, he deserves the treat.

In the end, it does not really matter how you exercise him. It should just give him stimulation, both mentally and physically. Play in an area that will avoid injuries for anyone and won't damage anything either. It can be hard to play inside a house with lots of breakables, so try taking him out once every day. It is ideal if you have your own lawn or backyard for him to enjoy. Make your dog's regular exercise a priority.

How to teach playing fetch

Playing fetch is one of the most enjoyable and simple activities to do with your dog. The retrieve command that you train him with will help you play this game easily. If you haven't taught him this yet, then do it. Use "fetch" as the cue word during this training. Show him that he has to go and catch the object that you threw and has to bring it back to you. Praise him every time he successfully carries it out and this will show him that he's doing it right. After this, every time you play fetch with him it will be a simple matter of throwing something out for him to get back to you. This game is especially for times when you don't really want to exert yourself physically too much by running or walking with him. Just show him a little enthusiasm by throwing the ball out, shouting fetch and praising him when he runs back to you with it. Just a smile on your face will be enough encouragement for him. Using his favorite toys in the beginning will make it easier for him to retrieve what you throw.

Catch a Frisbee

Games are the best way to entertain your dog and make him exercise as well. It is important to keep his body healthy by doing such exercises. One of the most fun games is playing with a Frisbee. It's a little harder than playing fetch with a ball or an object that stays in place. If your dog doesn't know how to play with a Frisbee, help him out at first by making him understand.

First, purchase a Frisbee that will be appropriate for playing with your dog. They bite into and chew most things so find a material that won't get ruined so fast. Also, try to find something that won't sink if it falls into water so your dog can still fetch it. Get a Frisbee that is durable and won't hurt anyone either.

Now, help your dog get familiar with the object. Let him see that it is his toy and for him to play with. Let him touch and smell it. Try playing tug of war with him with it before you start the Frisbee game. Make him reach for it from your hands, or keep it in a place and make him fetch it. Praise and reward him while he shows progress. First, start by rolling the disc on its side in the ground. He will naturally chase after it and grab it with his teeth. Make him fetch it back to you. Try these a few times. After these, try throwing the Frisbee in the air slowly and ask him to fetch it. Let him get familiarized to it, and soon he will be running and jumping at it. Slowly add height to your throws and let him enjoy chasing the Frisbee. This game is very energetic and will actually tire your dog out quite soon with all the running and jumping. Give him some water if he starts panting and let him rest. It is easy to teach a game of Frisbee to your dog and most kids enjoy this game with them as well.

Intro to Agility Training

Agility training is one of the more competitive forms of sport that is available for dogs. It involves obstacle courses with jumps and tunnels, etc. It is important for a dog and owner or handler to be in sync in order to train the dog properly. They need to learn how to navigate through these obstacles properly and without getting hurt. Agility training can simply be used as a form of exercise, while some enroll their dogs for actual competitions. Let your retriever first go through the trials. If they show that they can go through it without much difficulty, you can get them more involved in this training. You can enroll them in an agility-training institute or just set up some obstacles in your yard to enjoy with him.

Let your retriever start agility training at least after they are a year old. Basic obedience training is crucial before you enroll your dog in agility training. He should respond well to commands from you or anyone else. He should also be good at socializing with other people and dogs. Only then can he focus on learning how to pass these obstacle courses.

Teach him with contact obstacles like the teeter-totter, A-frame or the dog walk. These are called contact obstacles because at all times, at least one paw must be in contact with the obstacle. In the A-frame, your dog will learn to walk up a steep incline and then back down. This frame is shaped like a teepee. In the case of the dog walk, it is involving the dog walking on a balance beam. Teeter-totters for dogs are the same as those for humans. Start training by keeping everything at a low and easy level. Treat him when he does well.

Jumping obstacles are the next level. When you start training, keep the obstacles at a low height. Initially, they can injure themselves if they can't jump over it. Use command words to teach them if they have to make a short jump or a big jump. As they practice and gain confidence, dogs can easily jump over hurdles.

Tunnels are another part of an obstacle course for dogs. Start with a small tunnel that he can see through. If he can't see the end, he will be doubtful of entering. Slowly, he will get comfortable with moving through closed spaces and run through longer tunnels as well. Make sure the tunnel is wide enough for a big dog or he could get stuck in the middle and panic.

There are others like the Pause table and weave poles. Some obstacles take longer to master than others, and you shouldn't get impatient if you want your dog to try them. First, they need to learn to overcome each obstacle individually. When they master this, you can place a couple together and train him to go through these swiftly. Soon they will be able to complete a whole course without a single glitch.

If your dog is reluctant to try any type of obstacle, get him to watch other dogs first. Let him try those actions in an easy way that you set up. Don't force him to do anything. Let him get comfortable with it. With enough practice and praise, they will get the hang of it. Don't force him to do anything and don't try this for a dog that is too young, weak or sick. It needs extra effort and agility. There are many other forms of exercise that will do just fine for your retriever.

Conclusion

As you come to the end of this training guide, we would first like to thank you. We hope that it has proved useful and comprehensive in what you wanted to learn. Adopting a dog is almost always one of the best decisions you will make.

Golden retrievers, in particular, are one of the most lovable breeds around. They are very playful and a joy to have around. This is one of the reasons dogs are recommended as therapy for people who have depression. They can have a very calming and serene effect. It is actually quite easy to train retrievers. A little time and patience will go a long way. They are quick learners and, if taught well, they absorb it in their habits as well.

You need to always remember to be considerate of your dog and keep your behavior and actions in check. Do not try to assert yourself physically when you teach them something. It might be a little frustrating, but just let it be for a while and try again later. Your momentary anger can scar his spirit for a long time and this will make it harder for him to have trust in you. They are very sensitive so they respond well only to loving behavior.

If you want to be assertive, just a small change in tone will be enough to reprimand them. There is no need to shout or abuse them physically and it will give you the opposite of the result you were looking for. Instead, stay patient and use our tips to help you train your dog. Just go a day at a time and in a few weeks, they should be very easy to manage and be completely housetrained.

Golden retrievers are one of the most family-friendly animals that you can adopt and you will never regret it. If you find this book to be useful, go ahead and recommend it to any family or friends looking for help with training their own furry friends.

Now that you have all the information you need, the next and obvious step is to get started and start training your little pooch. It may not be an easy task, but I assure you, it will be extremely fun and will create an unbreakable bond between you and your dog. The end result will be so rewarding that you will be happy that you trained your dog on your own and didn't allow a stranger to take control of an important aspect, which is shaping their behavior.

I thank you once again for choosing this book and sincerely hope you find the experience of training your dog extremely fun and satisfying.

Golden Retriever Training Book for Beginners

Golden Retriever
Resources

Golden Retriever Breed Council

http://www.goldenretrievers.co.uk

Golden Retriever Club of America

https://www.grca.org

The Golden Retriever Club UK

https://thegoldenretrieverclub.co.uk

Golden Retriever Club Canada

https://grcc.net

Godlen Retriever Club of Scotland

www.goldenretrieverclubofscotland.com

American Kennel Club

https://www.akc.org/dog breeds/golden-retriever/

Golden Retriever Rescue

https://thegoldenretrieverclub.co.uk/rescue-page/